Your Calling as a Deacon

SEE ALSO

Your Calling as an Elder
Gary Straub

———————

Your Calling as a Leader
Gary Straub and Judy G. Turner

———————

Your Calling as a Christian
Timothy L. Carson

———————

Your Calling as a Teacher
Karen B. Tye

Your Calling
as a Deacon

Gary Straub
James Trader II

CHALICE
PRESS
ST. LOUIS, MISSOURI

Biblical quotations, unless otherwise noted, are from the *New Revised Standard Version Bible*, copyright 1989, Division of Christian Education of the National Council of the Churches of Christ in the United States of America. Used by permission. All rights reserved.

Quotations marked Message are from *The Message* by Eugene H. Peterson, copyright © 1993, 1994, 1995, 1996, 2000, 2001, 2002. Used by permission of NavPress Publishing Group. All rights reserved.

Cover and interior design: Elizabeth Wright

www.chalicepress.com

Print: 9780827244115
EPUB: 9780827244184   EPDF: 9780827244191

10 9 8 7 6   13 14 15 16 17

Library of Congress Cataloging–in–Publication Data

Straub, Gary.
  Your calling as a deacon / Gary Straub and James Trader II.
      p. cm.
  ISBN 978-0-827244-11-5 (pbk. : alk. paper)
  1. Deacons—Christian Church (Disciples of Christ) 2.
Christian Church (Disciples of Christ)—Government. I.
Trader, James. II. Title.
  BX7326.S77 2005
  262'.14663—dc22

                                        2004030148

Contents

Preface

When I wrote *Your Calling as an Elder* out on a rural retreat in Bald Knob, Kentucky, I had no idea about the potential impact. One unexpected, close-to-home impact was the declaration by a delegation of our indignant deacons: "So when are we going to do with deacons what we've done with elders?" This was a welcome word and fair question.

Isn't it time to dignify the office of deacon? After all the work being done these days to empower congregational elders, the deacons are not so quietly wondering, So what are we, chopped liver?

Unfortunately, the office of deacon is often treated as a brief stop on the road to becoming an elder. This treatment is a bad leadership move. It sends the wrong message about the ancient and honorable spiritual office and work of deacons. Let's be clear: Deacon's ministries are focused on a different dimension than elders. This does not make their efforts in any way inferior.

Future leadership in a postmodern era demands we define deacons as something more than elder wannabes. Being a deacon in tomorrow's church will require what Leonard Sweet calls E.P.I.C. effort. This is Sweet's way of imagining ministry that is: experiential, participatory, interactive, and connective. Deacons who practice this E.P.I.C. model of deaconing will have unique,

pioneering contributions to make to Christ's body in
the twenty-first century.[1]

A Special Dedication

Just a brief time before she died in the summer of
2004, Christian Board editorial director Jane McAvoy
tapped James Trader II, who has done some solid work
in the field of training the diaconate, to team with me
in what she imagined as "a companion piece to *Your
Calling As An Elder.*"

The three of us gathered in an empty classroom at
Lexington Seminary. After intently and politely listening
to James and me as we expounded on the ministry of
deacons, she began sketching out her vision of how
this book might unfold. I was astonished by her intuitive
grasp of the materials and keen insight. After a forty-
five-minute session of frantic data-entering, she closed
her laptop and treated us to lunch at a lunatic-fringe
type restaurant near the UK campus. We parted company,
never to see her again in this life. In appreciation of her
leadership, we have taken her guidance to heart and
tried to follow the path she set before us.

We own any straying from the vision she outlined,
even as we appreciatively dedicate this little volume to
Jane in gratitude for her original editorship. Thanks, Jane.

---

[1]Each of the authors has prepared and distributes a fuller workbook to
help deacons: James H. Trader II, *The Work of the Diaconate, A Training Program
for Deacons in the Christian Church (Disciples of Christ)* (Lexington, Ky.: LTS
Bookstore, 2000), consult ltsbookstore@lextheo.edu; and Gary Straub,
Discovering Your S.H.A.P.E. for Ministry (Frankfort, Ky.: First Christian Church),
consult WELLSPGS@aol.com.

1

Who Me, a Deacon?
Why Me?

Trust me—you're going to get this call. On the far end of the horizon of your cell phone, somebody from the nominating committee wants to know if you will serve as a deacon. Can you hear me now?

After you regain consciousness, you will want to know why they selected you. Maybe their thought process went something like the following:

Someone saw this deacon calling in you. They saw it when you spotted that single mom trying to fill three plates and juggle two kids in the potluck line after church. You found her a high chair, helped her brood get settled at a table, and introduced her around.

Someone noticed how you attend to the details of worship in such an efficient, easy way, smoothing the process and soothing the people.

Someone realized that when you say yes to a commitment in the life of the church, it is as good as done and done well.

Someone figured out that you don't wait to be asked. You take the initiative and meet the need. No fanfare or thanks needed.

Someone watched the way you led the youth group, including and appreciating each teen for his or her unique contribution to the project.

Obviously this mysterious someone "ratted you out" to the church nominating committee, prompting their call inviting you to consider becoming a deacon.

We're waiting; and your reaction to the call? That furtive look on your face, that cracked voice, that furrowed brow, that cold sweat; all scream that you are unprepared to respond. Before you launch that bogus spiel about "this is an obvious case of identity theft," take a 'time out,' will you?

Before you say no way, this little book welcomes you to consider thoughtfully and prayerfully the ancient and honorable office of Christian deacon. Instead of doing all the talking, take on the task of listening. Take a long look within; live attentively. Pay attention to the silent side of prayer.

Now, I will grant you that some churches just need "warm bodies" to fill deacon slots, complete rosters, present a full slate, and stack committees. In that case your "calling" will consist of frantic activity without much spiritual focus, busy work. In churches trying to fill slots, the invitation to become a deacon may not mean much. But let's not go there!

Instead, consider deaconing to be your next spiritual adventure, a chance to explore who you are before God and to serve a purpose beyond yourself. Let's explore this possibility. Spiritual adventures often unfold at "hinge" moments for the soul. Hinge moments happen when we are willing to hold ourselves open to God and deeply listen to what our lives are telling us. In hinge moments the door between time and eternity swings wide open into an unexplored dimension.

I don't mean to make your calling as a deacon sound like an episode of *The Twilight Zone.* I was hoping your calling as a deacon might serve as a wake-up call. You are done mushing your way through the mundane. You are off on an adventure with God.

As you hold in your heart the possibility that God is up to something in your life, I invite you into a season of thoughtful discernment. Carve out some intentional moments of reflection. I don't mean take a thirty-day silent retreat with the Benedictines. You might be surprised at what can happen in fifteen minutes.

Ready or not, plop down in your favorite chair and light a candle to symbolize your desire for illumination. Focus your attention on your breathing and center yourself. Offer to God your intention to become open. Sometimes when the distractions of daily life are distressing you, it requires great effort to still your soul. As you give less energy to the distraction and more energy to being present to Christ, an almost imperceptible shift takes place. You begin to notice moments of God's presence, power, and love. In this moment, ask God what this invitation to become a deacon means at this point in your life and at this season in your lifelong discipleship. Sometimes new spiritual adventures signal the cutting edge of our growth toward Christ. Take a deep breath. As you exhale, rest at the bottom of your breath and listen to any nuance or nudge the Spirit may be offering you. Lift your gratitude to God for all that it means to even be asked to serve as a deacon. Trust the promise that where God guides, God also provides. Claim the faith that whatever wisdom necessary to make a solid discernment will be yours as you explore this call.

Discernment is about holding your life up to God, offering your gratitude for guidance, and listening as if your life depended on it, because it does! There, now you've started. That wasn't so hard after all!

Attraction to Distraction in Listening for a Call

Dealing with your inward attraction to distraction is not always easy when seeking to listen to God in prayer. The almost magnetic pull toward mind clutter and a noisy heart may be refocused by choosing to intentionally work your way through these fourteen focal factors as you process your own discernment. You may want to use them, one by one, as a resting place for your spirit.

1. Fear Factor

   This is your time to exaggerate and awful-ize. Imagine your worst nightmare about being a deacon. Own up to this anxiety however dreadful, silly, or inappropriate. This is no time for being proper and polite. Know that confessing this fear begins to tame it. Often, courage is just fear that has said its prayers!

2. Unfinished Factor

   New levels of spiritual responsibility have a way of jogging our psyche and surfacing unfinished business that has been buried beneath the busyness. Are there emotional, spiritual, or personal issues so unattended and unaddressed internally as to hinder my ability to effectively serve? Do I have hot button issues that blind, distort, and impair my judgment? Instead of dealing with my own unfinished soul work, do I project internal problems onto others, assuming they have the problem? What must I do to be finished with this past, so I can fully consider God's preferred future for me? Do I have any earthly idea what a positive resolution would even look like?

3. Scandal Factor

   Could anything in my life create a scandal to the gospel and hand non-Christians a "free pass" to disrespect the church? If I am in the recovery process, am I recognized by my peers as being far enough along to guide others? Is my life in order? Are there any skeletons in my closet that would cause the church embarrassment? Of course we all have some, but this refers to public things like arrests, felonies, lawsuits, violations, and accusations that might negatively impact the church's witness. How was the matter disposed of? How long ago is "long enough" ago? Is the shadowy side of my life surrendered to the Spirit? Do I need some wise counsel? Whom can I trust to confidentially discuss these matters?

4. Joy Factor

Can I name the joy that leaps within when I consider this call? Sometimes a collision occurs at the intersection of your deep joy and the world's great need. This is the kind of cosmic collision that often accompanies a call. After sweeping all the dark corners of our lives for cobwebs, how delightful it is to simply acknowledge the sheer joy of being of any service to our Creator, Sustainer, and Redeemer God.

5. Devotion Factor

Have I sufficiently attended to my inner life and developed habits of the heart and spiritual practices that sustain me in tough times? Do I have anything to offer souls who are fed up, used up, burned up, burned out, and bummed out? Do my practices feed my own soul and provide a wellspring of spiritual strength to draw upon? Do I know how to dwell in Christ? Can I sustain myself and serve others over the long haul?

6. Gift Factor

   Have I discovered my own spiritual gifts? Do I even know what they are? Do I have an inkling of how they operate? Am I willing to work through a process to uncover them so I can offer them effectively in Christ's service? How might my strengths be teamed with others to complement the ministry needs of the congregation for this season of our life together as a faith community?

7. Fun Factor

   God's work is not *all* deadly drudgery! What would make deaconing fun for me? Do opportunities to learn excite me? Does the prospect of spiritual growth sound like fun? Would getting to hang out with people I admire and appreciate strengthen my desire to serve? Where is the fun in this call? If you aren't drawn to a fun factor, don't do it; you'll drag the whole team down!

8. Pastor Factor

   Do I have a positive personal regard for the pastoral staff? Am I open to working closely with them? Is there a sincere spirit of collegiality among us? If not, am I willing to do my part to heal and reconcile this key relationship? We may not have a personal friendship, but do we at least have a solid basis for mutual respect? Can I support my pastor and trust that she or he will support me? Am I willing to lead and be led by my pastor and/or pastoral staff?

9. Example Factor

Will I be able to deal comfortably with the expectation of being looked up to as a spiritual example in behavior and attitude? If being a role model makes me nervous, can I at least imagine myself growing into this role? Am I able to claim my own Christlikeness without resorting to false piety or lapsing into denial of the power that God has given me to offer others? Am I comfortable with my own spiritual seasoning and maturation? Do I understand the principle that people are only looking through me to Christ?

10. Legacy Factor

What difference might my service make for the church's coming generations? What spiritual and material resources can I offer to God in a way that provides a legacy, a gift, for the years beyond my own lifetime? Creating an example of how to move beyond success to spiritual significance for Christ in the generations yet-to-come is a powerful positive motivator. Blazing a trail for others to follow might mean that I will need to be much more intentional about stewarding my resources to maximize future impact. Leaving a legacy requires looking for creative ways to extend the kingdom's purpose beyond my lifetime.

11. Shadow Factor

Count on deaconing to bring us nose-to-nose and face-to-face with our own faults, frailties, flaws, foibles, finitude, and fragility. If we can't see them, someone else will be glad to point out all the dreadful specifics. Relax! Everybody has a shadow side to his or her personality; it's part of being human. We can't always predict the outcome when the shadow side of our soul emerges. We can, however, submit ourselves to God and surrender to the Spirit. Paul's "thorn in the flesh" was never removed, but he discovered "I can do all things through him (Christ) who strengthens me" (Phil. 4:13). Perhaps we have this treasure in such "earthen vessels," so the excellence of the power shining through the cracks may be God's and not a reflection of us!

12. Cost Factor

King David said, "I will not offer burnt offerings to the LORD my God that cost me nothing" (2 Sam. 24:24). Jesus advised his disciples to count the cost before committing to follow when he said, "No one who puts a hand to the plow and looks back is fit for the kingdom of God" (Lk. 9:62). How do I calculate the cost of being a deacon? What am I willing to pay to follow the Christ who gave his all? Two seldom-used words come to mind: obedience and sacrifice. Calculating these costs may save you some bellyaching later!

13. Faith Factor

Are the spiritual allegiances of my life solidly in place? Can I honestly claim the core teachings of Christianity well enough to embody them effectively in my daily life and practices? Am I knowledgeable enough to at least informally teach them? If the answer is no, then am I willing to commit to a course of spiritual learning to improve major deficiencies? Once I get beyond me, am I willing to answer the call to step out in faith and help lead the way? John said it best: "This is the victory that conquers the world, our faith" (1 Jn. 5:4).

14. Vision Factor

Not everybody is a visionary. (Thank God!) If I am not a seer of dreams and visions, do I at least recognize such a leader when I see one? Am I a valuable follower and contributor? Never discount the power of positive support and a can-do spirit. Can I be comfortable experiencing someone else's vision and finding my unique part within that framework? Do I have a personal mission statement? How does God's mission for me dovetail with the congregation's vision at this time?

I hope you will carry these fourteen factors around in your heart for a while before saying yes or no. It may become important to you that you hollow out a little more space to "walk the furrowed fields of your mind" before God. You may find it helpful to take a day retreat around these focal points along with scripture reading and a bit of reflective journaling. Some folks can't know for certain what they think until they see it written out on a piece of paper! Many active minds discover prayer-walking settles them into a quieter place with God. Sometimes, embracing and loving the question is answer enough; at other times we feel the need for something as specific as a sign. My own sense of it is that anyone who loves God enough to earnestly seek God's guidance will be found by the needed grace.

So Really, Why *Did* They Ask You to Be a Deacon?

Beyond believing you would enjoy the awesome honor of serving Christ's church as a deacon, what else may have prompted the nominating committee's call?

Consider this: You may have been selected to serve as a deacon because they recognized that you already are one! I like to encourage those charged with calling out our next generation of leaders to look out across the life of our congregation and ask, who is already deaconing? You came up on the radar screen because you are already displaying the most critical ingredient in a deacon's heart, a serving spirit. You have already displayed and demonstrated the servant's heart of Christ to someone, or your name wouldn't have even come up.

Let's face it. Being a deacon is not like winning a church popularity contest. It's not like being named Mr. or Ms. Congeniality at the state fair! The title *deacon* is not handed out as a reward for distinguished giving. It certainly is not offered as an incentive to reactivate a member whose attendance and interest in church is somewhat lagging.

You are called to be a deacon because your life *already* bears the marks of willing service to Christ's kingdom. You *are* one! To put it bluntly what you would not even think about doing for love or money you would gladly do if obedience to Christ clearly called for that act of service. You are a devoted servant of the servant heart of Christ. This is not an "on-again/off-again, occasional, if-I'm-in-a-good-mood-and-feel-like-it" thing with you. This is no mere whim or fancy! This is your heartbeat. You are an enthusiastic, passionate follower of Christ, who *is* your life.

A Few Words of Order

Some congregations use a rotational system of deacons. A person serves for several years on the official administrative board and committees and then rotates off for a year. A deacon can elect, if asked, to return to active service for another term. These days, many congregations have streamlined their top-heavy organizational chart. They make being on or off the administrative board a totally separate experience from continuing service as a deacon in one of the congregation's ministries. Often in such congregations, deacons are installed for a lifetime of active service and may request a sabbatical for rest, rejuvenating, and retooling for future opportunities of service. Being elected to the administrative board is no longer automatically linked to a deacon's ongoing ministry of service.

If You Are a Returning Deacon...

Congratulations! You are off the bench and back in the game! If, while you were on the sidelines, changes were made in the game plan, graciously try to accommodate new ways. If not, seek counsel and voice your concerns in a way that respects the fact that the church's life and ministry go on with or without us. Even how you go about inquiring and questioning can be an example of positive leadership. If your enthusiasm for previous tasks has waned, don't hesitate to step up to new opportunities or to help create new ministries. Not only what you do but the spirit with which you do it can make all the difference in your congregation. If there are new faces in leadership, get to know them. Hear their dreams, know their hearts, and find your place in this fresh season of service. As you reflect on previous stints of service, ask yourself, what one dumb thing do I need to stop doing that could quite possibly improve my deaconing by 80 percent?

If You Are a Newly-minted Deacon...

Congratulations! You have no idea what you have gotten yourself into, do you? Yet you have joined the ranks of an ancient and honorable order of servants who hark back to those halcyon New Testament times when the Spirit was molding Christ's body on earth and when deacons were a critical component in his work.

Your initial anxiety over whether or not you are worthy to be a deacon is completely normal. If you did not have some jitters or self-questioning, the nominating committee might not have done a thorough job in explaining your new role. You are being asked to step out of the pews, out of the rank and file, to honor Christ's body by becoming the servant of the servants of Christ. Strange as it may seem to you on the front end, the higher you are called in the church's offices, the more people you serve and carry in love. Henri Nouwen once alluded to this concept in a lecture as the inverted triangle of service.[1] Becoming a deacon is not so much a promotion to a "higher rank" as it is a wider opportunity to offer ministry. Nervousness will

---

[1] Henri J. M. Nouwen, *Reminder: Service and Prayer in Memory of Jesus Christ* (San Francisco: Harper SanFrancisco, 1998), 1.

soon give way to the sheer joy of getting to be present in sacred moments when people's souls are touched, comforted, and challenged. You get to help make a difference.

2

Deacons in the New Testament

The office of deacon is probably first noted within the book of Acts, specifically Acts 6:2–9 (compare 8:26–38). Seven were chosen, among them Stephen, to handle the responsibilities that the twelve apostles did not feel called to. Deacons' appointments came as a response to the complaint that the widows were being neglected in the daily distribution of food.

Irenaeus, bishop of Lyons, writing about 185 C.E. was probably the first to call Stephen a deacon. He seems to have taken the word directly from the Greek word *diakonos*, meaning "a table waiter" or "servant." References in Philippians and First Timothy show that by the mid 60s C.E. the office of deacon was part of the church's servant life. Acts refers to deacons serving as evangelists and witnesses.

First Timothy 3:8–13 continues the list of characteristics from the book of Acts for a deacon and sets the standard for those who would serve in that capacity. This passage is clear that the office of deacon is fulfilled not only by men but by women as well. Paul, in Romans 16, makes reference to Phoebe as a deacon. The deacon of the second century C.E. saw to the physical needs of the congregation and was a valued assistant to the one who presided.

Aside from the characteristics asserted in the book of Acts and First Timothy, the New Testament offers little information about the role of the deacon in the church.

The Church's Tradition

Within the tradition of the church a deacon was an assistant to the one who presided, usually called a bishop. In the understanding of the church at the time the bishop was the equivalent of a minister or priest today. The deacon could generally

1. Serve with or in the place of the bishop by officiating at all religious ceremonies, baptizing (on commission from the bishop), preaching, reading Scripture, gathering and administering funds, assisting in distributing communion, and ministering to the sick.

2. Serve as liaison between the bishop and the congregation, keeping the bishop aware of the personal and spiritual needs of the flock and at the

same time informing the congregation of the vision of the bishop and of their dutiful response to his leadership.

3. Serve as usher when the bishop presided at worship.
4. Serve as scribe and secretary to the bishop.[1]

In the fourth century C.E. the Council of Arles denied the deacon the right to serve communion. By 380 the Council of Nicea placed the deacon at the bottom of the list under bishop and presbyter or priest. The deacon was given the role of overseer of the physical needs of the congregation.[2]

Little is known about the diaconate between 700 C.E. and the Protestant Reformation except that the office served as a stepping-stone for the priesthood. Protestant churches reexamined the roles of the deacons and considered what their usefulness in the Protestant structure might be. Myriad understandings came about. Some churches see the deacon as one step to becoming a priest. Others have retained the role of table server, while others have employed deacons in specialized ministries, such as working with homebound members; maintaining houses of worship; ministering to the poor, the widowed, and the orphaned; or seeing to the social ministries of the church. Within the Christian Church

---

[1]*One Diaconate, Women and Men Building a Community of Service and Ministry* (St. Louis: Christian Board of Publication, 1996), 20.
[2]Ibid., 22.

(Disciples of Christ) almost all these understandings can be found.[3]

A Deacon Is a Deacon Is a Deacon...or Not

Imagine going into a hardware store and asking for a hammer and being handed a screwdriver or possibly even a wheelbarrow. At their most basic level each of these is a tool, yet they serve completely different purposes. Although many churches retain the office of deacon, they often mean different things by the term. What is clear is that in each of these churches' definitions the model of servanthood is at the core.

Within the Roman Catholic and Episcopal churches the deacon is a member of the clergy. Deacons may fulfill most of the functions of the priest but are generally assigned to assist the priest.[4] In each tradition some deacons are permanent, absolute, or perpetual deacons, while some deacons are transitional deacons, deacons who intend to be ordained as priests.[5]

The different branches of the Lutheran Church have a number of understandings of the office of deacon. In some congregations deacons may be considered clergy,

---

[3]Ibid., 30.

[4]Gerhard Berghoef and Lester DeKoster, *The Deacon's Handbook, A Manual of Stewardship* (Grand Rapids, Mich.: Christian's Library Press, 1980), 75.

[5]James Monroe Barnett, *The Diaconate, A Full and Equal Order* (Valley Forge, Pa.: Trinity Press International, 1995), 148.

but in most the diaconate is a lay ministry. The church continues ongoing conversation about this issue.[6]

Generally, within the Presbyterian Church the diaconate is responsible for the physical needs of the church. Deacons are in charge of or a part of most of the committees of the church. They are the stewards of both the money and the property and see to the physical needs of those within the congregation, particularly the sick and those in need. Their most visible duties are probably serving as ushers at services and events within the church.[7] Baptist churches evidence many understandings of the role of the deacons. In most the deacon fulfills a role similar to that of the elder in the Christian Church (Disciples of Christ). The board of deacons is often the policy-making body of the church. They see to the physical and spiritual needs of the members, the property, and the pastor.[8] In some Baptist churches deacons are ordained for life, but in others they serve for limited periods of time.[9]

The United Methodist Church no longer has a transitional diaconate. Diaconal ministers are often ordained to specific ministries.

---

[6]Ibid., 157–58.

[7]Andrew A. Jumper, *Chosen to Serve, The Deacon, Presbyterian Church in the United States* (Richmond, Va.: John Knox Press, 1961), 9–14.

[8]F.A. Agar, *The Deacon at Work* (Philadelphia, Boston: Judson Press, 1923), 39–40.

[9]Barnett, *The Diaconate*, 160–61.

The United Church of Christ, as a congregational church, is as likely to have a board of deacons as not. The duties of deacons range from responsibilities in worship to the care of the members. Typically, within the UCC the office of deacon is not considered an office in the historic sense.[10]

The office of deacon is obviously not the same for each denomination, nor is it the same in individual churches within the congregationally governed denominations. Despite the variety of understandings about certain details, most churches perceive the primary role of deacons as that of servants. The deacon's responsibilities invariably include seeing to the physical needs of the church and the members.

If the Shoes Fit, Why Do My Feet Hurt?

You may be wondering if you truly fit the job description when you read the qualifications for deacons in 1 Timothy 3:8–13. Most of us know how uncomfortable it is to be responsible for something that we're unprepared for. It's much like trying to wear shoes that are too big, or worse, too small. We must realize that the list in First Timothy is a dream list. No individual person will ever be able to fulfill perfectly all the qualifications listed there. What is important is that we strive to be the best at each of these qualifications,

----

[10]Ibid., 163.

to understand the gifts we do have, and to use them in the best ways possible.

As amazing as the varieties of gifts of human beings may be, it is absolutely astounding how people have tried to limit the number and type of acceptable gifts. Because of the masculine language in much of scripture, women have throughout history been excluded from church offices or separated from men in their own group. As we saw above, Paul in Romans 16 makes specific mention of Phoebe's carrying out the role of a deacon, and the description of the deacon in First Timothy is clear about the inclusion of women in the body of deacons. However, even in many Disciples churches women were often separated from deacons and given the title deaconesses. The book *One Diaconate, Women and Men Building a Community of Service and Ministry,* originally published in the 1970s, helped many congregations to merge these separate groups into a single diaconate. However, a few Disciples congregations still maintain a male-only diaconate. Others use the gifts of women only in the preparation of communion, not in the serving it.

Many of the qualifications listed have been used to exclude individuals from the diaconate. Some will argue that deacons must be married because the scripture says that deacons should be married only once. Paul was probably talking more about polygamy than about singles or divorcees. If Paul were specifically talking about the singleness of the deacon, he would then contradict himself in First Corinthians, where he suggests that it is best for Christians in general to not be married because that could divide one's loyalties to God and serve as a distraction to one's true tasks.

Some have tried to suggest that when Paul says that the deacon should be serious (or earnest or grave), he means that humor has no place within the church, an absurd understanding at best. If this were true, most of Jesus' parables wouldn't work as teaching tools. Humor is not the opposite of seriousness. A better antonym would be frivolity. Obsession with the pursuit of frivolous activities separates us from God and service to others.

Another qualification used to disqualify persons is the instruction to not indulge in too much wine. This is often read as a call to be teetotalers. Indeed, many people have difficulty when it comes to substance abuse, but as with any other thing that separates us from God and one another, those who are able to practice in moderation should not be excluded from serving God. Even those who are recovering alcoholics or addicts may serve, provided they have recognized the addiction, have sought treatment, and are sufficiently mature in the recovery process.

Many of the qualifications are necessary not just for deacons but for Christians as well. Having maturity; being filled with faith, the Spirit, and wisdom; and understanding one's faith and tradition should be part of every Christian's life and journey. Likewise, we hope that all Christians strive to be good managers of their children and their households. Still, deacons must be especially careful on these points. After all, these are the people to whom we are entrusting the people and property of the church.

It's not difficult to see that a deacon should not be covetous or greedy. Serving others and wanting everything for yourself are about as incompatible as it gets. The stumbling blocks for servants, though, are not in the material things. Those in service often covet recognition and honors. This type of greed most often gets in the way of the servant's tasks. It may not be obvious, but for the servant who fulfills duties to God and church, the service is the reward.

One of the "givens" of the church meeting is the meeting that occurs minutes later in the parking lot. Some would say that more is actually accomplished in these meetings. One of the problems with these meetings, though, is that as the previous meeting is reviewed and dissected, the conversation turns to gossip and backbiting. Sadly, we often see someone's true nature at times like these. Deacons are called not to be double-tongued. Speaking ill of others, repeating gossip, and not telling the whole truth are all part of the problem. The deacon should try to avoid these behaviors and attempt to curb these behaviors in others. Refusing to participate in such activities takes strength and courage, but the end result is usually respect.

As hard as it may be to believe, we are often guilty of finding reasons to exclude people from serving God, even referring to scripture for our justification. If any of us were to be examined with such withering scrutiny, no one would be left to serve. God has gifted us all, and we are all called to respond to the grace of those gifts by using them in service to God through serving the people of God.

CAN A FLY PARTAKE OF COMMUNION?

A small Kentucky congregation has a deacon who is developmentally disabled. As he was serving communion to the pastor one Sunday morning, he whispered to her that she shouldn't take the cup she was reaching for because there was a fly in it. Stifling her smile, she thanked him and took another cup. Many of us would have removed the cup and placed it somewhere out of the way until after the service, but his solution was just as valid. By warning his pastor of the offending insect, he showed that he understood his duty and took his care of the people in the congregation seriously.

Developmental disabilities, handicaps both visible and hidden, and even the prejudices we have about those with speech impediments or heavy accents have kept many people from serving God to the best of their abilities. Although persons with disabilities may not be able to fulfill all the duties the diaconate is called upon to perform, they can probably perform some tasks. A disability should not be used to exclude someone from service even if reasonable accommodations need to be made.

Many persons confined to beds or wheelchairs have telephones with automatic dialers and would be perfectly willing to participate in phone trees or prayer chains or to contact members with announcements or concerns.

Those who have difficulty speaking may be able to handle physical tasks easily and vice versa.

Mentally challenged individuals, even those with severe retardation, may be able to handle simple tasks such as cleanup or preparation of communion. In fact, once trained in these tasks, they are often quite focused and perform them willingly and with great determination.

God calls everyone! That's about as inclusive as it gets. Everyone, not just those whole in body, mind, and spirit, is called to serve God by serving others. Everyone is a child of God, and everyone inherits an equal share of the kingdom. And when you get to the bottom of things, everyone has a disability of some sort.

3

The Heart of a Deacon

Acts 6 describes the role and qualifications of deacons as the need was first discerned and called forth in the life of the early church. Did you notice that the office of deacon arose out of a conflict? Both the numbers of those cared for by the church's benevolence and the quality of their care were being jeopardized by the way the apostles were (dis)organized to handle the ministry. This gave rise to accusations that Hebrew widows were being favored above widows of other nationalities. The creative energy of God flowing in their midst solved the problem. An occasion for bitterness became an opportunity for betterment and ministry growth as the first deacons were appointed. The major spiritual qualification appears to be twofold: "full of faith and the Holy Spirit" (Acts 6:5). This dual devotion rules the heart of the deacons' role and ministry in New Testament times.

Reflecting on that text, I keep coming back to the words of Henri Nouwen in his simple book, *The Living Reminder: Service and Prayer in Memory of Jesus Christ*. Nouwen intuitively perceived that "there is only one ministry in the whole wide world; that of Jesus Christ."[1] All any of us ever does (no matter who we are or think we are) is re-present that once and yet forever ministry of Christ. We stand in his place for others; representing God's presence, power, and love. Deacons are to be transformed continuously by Christ and thus become Christ for others. What an extraordinary privilege!

Applying Nouwen's concept to the work of deacons, we recognize this principle at work in the upper room. Jesus graphically illustrates to the reluctant disciples that serving one another is serving God. John's upper room insights (Jn. 13:3–11) provide a guiding image that touches to the core of deacons' work. In the midst of supper, between courses, Jesus rose from table because some critical need had been left unattended. Quite un–self-consciously, Jesus laid aside his outer garments and took a towel and tied it around his waist. Pouring water into a basin, he began to work his way around the foot of the reclining couches, washing each disciple's dusty feet as he went and wiping them with the towel wrapped around his waist.

---

[1]Henri J. M. Nouwen *Living Reminder: Service and Prayer in Memory of Jesus Christ* (San Francisco: Harper SanFrancisco, 1998).

Jesus' act was, to say the least, a shocking breach of household etiquette. No one even had to consult Dear Abby to know this job was not appropriate for the guest of honor. Foot washing was an ugly task reserved for the lowliest servant in the pecking order. No wonder Peter was anxious when Jesus came to the spot where he was reclining! Even Mr. Uncouth sensed something was dreadfully out of order. Flustered, Peter flatly refused to have anything to do with this whole scenario. The job Jesus took on was a nasty but most necessary act of hospitality if the disciples were to be appropriately clean for full participation in the banquet and worship of Passover. Only upon completing this ritual cleansing were guests fully qualified to share in the glorious feast commemorating freedom.

When the ritual is complete, the "audio portion" that goes with the "video piece" of this passage is equally instructive. Jesus' words "I've laid down a pattern for you" (Jn. 13:15, *Message*) is not literally about ordaining an annual foot-washing service. Jesus is lifting up the servant-leader lifestyle and commending it to his frightened followers. "So if I, your Lord and Teacher, have washed your feet, you also ought to wash one another's feet…If you know these things, you are blessed if you do them." (Jn. 13:14, 17) It's clear that deacons are to be "doers of the word, and not merely hearers" (Jas. 1:22). Deacons must be the embodied word of God for others, the 'good book' others can read and pattern their life after.

Jesus blesses his clueless companions with an over-arching metaphor for the life and service of a deacon. Deacons are members of the ancient and honorable "Order of the Towel and Basin." Deacons do whatever needs to be done to prepare and present God's people for God's service. Servants of the servants; deacons are nothing more, nothing less, and nothing else!

Imagine! By our humble acts of service, we qualify people; we present people, we assist in preparing them fully for the feast of freedom that completely liberates and brings the life of God to life in them! By taking up the basin and towel, we assist in their passing into the full life of God through Christ. In his servant heart, Jesus longed for God's children sitting in that upper room that night to enter into and experientially know the saving power of God's mighty deeds. He wanted them to have more than just a nodding acquaintance with the history of how the Hebrew children miracu-lously passed through the Red Sea. He wanted them individually and personally to experience their very own beloved Christ's passing over from death to life.

Did you notice how Jesus got their undivided attention? He didn't raise his voice. Nor did he do something theatrically spectacular like balancing an elephant on a golf ball. He didn't even preach, lecture, or entertain! He performed a stark and startling act of humble service so strikingly beneath his dignity that it was painfully embarrassing even for Peter, the most thickheaded, socially inept, stubborn, and insensitive among them. This humility is what Paul speaks of in Philippians 2:5–8: "Let the same mind be in you that was in Christ Jesus, who, though he was in the form of God, did not regard equality with God as something to be exploited, but emptied himself, taking the form of a slave, being born in human likeness. And being found in human form, he humbled himself and became obedient to the point of death—even death on a cross."

Mel Gibson's movie *The Passion of Christ* pushed us to confront the confounding fact that crucifixion was the ugliest and most undignified, debasing, and shameful form of death in the known world. Christ's single-minded purpose to serve God's will, even if it meant inglorious death, helps us test the outer limits of our spiritual commitment, too.

Deacons, have you allowed the implications of Christ's humility to hit you yet? If Jesus' servant heart hushed and humbled Peter, the brassiest of braggarts, how does it shape our ministry? What do you notice about Christ's ego? Of course he had an ego, or he could not have negotiated his relationships. But Jesus did not live by an ego-driven agenda. His ego was not self-congratulatory and self-serving. Christ's ego was operative in his personality but "out of the way," so the power of his deepest self, connected in quiet communion with the heart of God, could shine through. Where does that lead us in the realm of service?

Somehow, Jesus lived by the inverse principle of leadership. The higher you rise in the life of the kingdom, the more people you quietly carry and humbly serve in love. All those who practice their faith as deacons and serve out of the servant heart of Christ catch the fire of this enormous power. All the great servants of the heart of Christ through the ages, from Francis of Assisi to Mother Teresa to Archbishop Romero to Dietrich Bonhoeffer to Martin Luther King Jr. to the most obscure, unknown saint, knew this liberating truth and struggled to hold body and soul together only so they could continue to serve. We live out of the servant heart of Christ.

Please understand, I do not mean to imply in this humility some wimpy, martyrlike groveling. You know the kind I mean? The old "that's all right, you take the big pork chop, and I'll eat this dirt. Don't worry about me; I'll be all right!" Not an ounce of the energy of Christ is in this cheesy, self-debasing, "roll-over-and-play-dead" attitude. Self-abnegation is overrated, because in the end, life should be about Christ. We need to embody a healthy, loving, and fully aware yet intentionally sacrificial lifestyle that is in keeping with Christ's own choice to live for others, not just himself.

At the heart of every vibrant congregation is a dedicated core of deacons who are living out of the joys of Christ's own servant heart.

4

Discerning our Gifts
as Deacons

Deacons are, by and large, open-hearted and eager souls, quite willing and able. Much of the actual work in our congregations is done by deacons who have already put in a full day's work by the time they get to church. Talk about exemplary dedication. Congregations are blessed by the benefit of their leadership.

Beyond simply honoring deacons' dedication to their calling, we need to be concerned with what sustains the service of deacons. We raise the question of staying power because burnout is evident among deacons, creating major morale problems at the grassroots of our congregations. Perhaps we are working hard but not smart. Perhaps we too often fill slots to complete rosters and appoint warm bodies to committees with little thought as to a deacon's spiritual gifts or what it might look like to build ministry teams based on a mix of spiritual gifts that complement instead of compete.

Because our spiritual heritage as Disciples favors a highly rationalistic approach to faith, we are generally uncomfortable with references to the Holy Spirit. Sadly, we associate the work of the Spirit with the emotional excesses of frontier revivalism at its worst. Make no mistake, revivalism has a ridiculous side still claimed by television evangelists.

Can we get beyond caricatures and stereotypes? Let's get back to the biblical teaching of our heritage. Disciples have long believed that the Spirit is active in the human soul by reason of God's Spirit breathing divine life into us at creation (Gen. 2:7). So we are born of the dust, with our God-destiny infused into us by the breath of God. This spark of the Divine manifests itself through enthusiasm, derived from the Latin, meaning "in God." We breathe in the breath of God through the Holy Spirit.

In John 3 in conversation with Nicodemus Jesus says we are "born from above," referring to the second birth. He means we are born again by the breath of the Holy Spirit. But the reception of this Spirit is not necessarily some rare mystical experience only available to those who are secretly initiated. Far from being some exclusive experience only open to a few spiritually elite, Disciples teach that all believers receive the Holy Spirit as the indwelling presence of God at the moment of baptism.

Historically, Disciples have quoted Acts 2:38 as the key verse in our understanding of salvation. "Repent, and be baptized every one of you in the name of Jesus Christ so that your sins may be forgiven; and you will receive the gift of the Holy Spirit." We focus our attention on the baptismal emphasis, ignoring the apostolic teaching regarding the inception of the Holy Spirit. In the moment of baptism, spirits human and Holy commingle and commune. The divine spark that every living soul receives at birth now becomes the indwelling Spirit whom Jesus promised would "guide you into all the truth" (Jn. 16:13). Thus the Spirit makes us strong followers "rooted and grounded in love," according to Ephesians 3:14–19.

With the Spirit as our anchor and guide, we begin to grow spiritually. Our minds begin to take on the considerations of Christ's mind (Phil 2:5). Conscience becomes sensitized by the concern to discern what is of the spirit and what is of the flesh. (Rom. 7:14—8:17.) The development of our spiritual character ensues as our "suffering produces endurance, and endurance produces character, and character produces hope, and hope does not disappoint us, because God's love has been poured into our hearts through the Holy Spirit that has been given to us" (Rom. 5:3–5).The fruits of the Spirit (Gal 5:22–23) are another way of talking about this internal re-vitalization process. Fruits of the Spirit are essentially manifestations of Christ's life shining through our lives: his character, his compassion, his quiet strength, his courage in danger. All these graces become ours as we open ourselves up and welcome the Holy Spirit to commune with our spirit in the depths our being. The light of Christ within us shines ever more brightly, even through cracks and crevices of our souls. Paul reminds us that "we have this treasure [of the Divine Life] in earthen vessels, that the excellency of the power may be of God, and not of us" (2 Cor. 4:7, KJV).

A progression of this spiritual growth can be summarized like this: We are *rooted* in the soil of God's Spirit, *fruited* to manifest the mind and heart of Christ, then *gifted* for kingdom service.

Spiritual gifts are unmerited blessings from God. The saving grace of Christ is the same for all, but the serving grace is shaped around our unique reflections of the image of God. Gifts are special powers or abilities given by God to build up the body of Christ. Gifts are essentially job descriptions for ministries. God wills the world to be whole and for the gifts to serve God's purpose (2 Cor. 5:18–20). The presence of Christ is known through the exercise of our gifts (Eph. 4:12–16) The threefold purpose of gifts is: (1) to build up the body of Christ (1 Cor.12:27, 14:12, and 14:26, 1 Peter 4:10); (2) to serve to reconcile the world and minister healing and blessing (Rom. 12:2–8 and 1 Cor. 12:7); and (3) to honor and glorify God, the Giver of all gifts (Jas. 1:17).

Certainly it is critical to our discipleship as deacons that we discover and use our spiritual gifts (1 Cor.12:1). We will not only herein discover our individual purpose in life but also find fulfillment in rightful use of the gifts (Rom. 12:1–2; Jn. 15:8, 10–11; Eph. 4:11–15).

Because there has been so much controversy over the proper use of gifts, perhaps some perspective might help. First, Disciples are definitely charismatic people! I do not mean that in some slick, sales-gimmicky way. We are gifted in the biblical sense. The Greek word *charis* means gift. Given this understanding, all Christians are charismatic. Why give away a perfectly good word to the Pentecostals? If someone asks, "are you charismatic?" your final answer is yes. You are indeed gifted, and your giftedness is not intended to enhance your ego or exalt a personal agenda. Gifts are spiritual power for building up the kingdom of God, not to be squandered on selfish ends.

Second, we often lose sight of the fact that embodying Christ's love is more important than all the gifts combined. We often overlook the fact that Paul's famous love chapter (1 Cor. 13) is placed in the middle of his teaching on the exercise of spiritual gifts (1 Cor. 12 and 14). The Corinthian passages along with Romans 12 and Ephesians 4 are worthy subjects for a deacon's Bible study.

Third, because the names and exact number of gifts vary in these passages, you may find it more helpful to not consider them exhaustive or exclusive. For instance, some people have the spiritual gift of irritation. They state matters in such a provocative way that they spur and inspire completion of tasks long past due. I don't see this gift in any New Testament listing, but exercising motivation (even if sometimes somewhat "offensive") is quite necessary for today's church. Or consider the case with martyrdom, which can only be exercised once! I also exclude tongue-speaking along with snake-handling in the working list of gifts, because neither are exercised much in mainline church settings.

Fourth, the key to discovering your gifts is to be clear on the goal in seeking the gifts: servanthood. Nothing more. Nothing else. Nothing less.

I encourage you to launch the discovery of your spiritual gifts by working with the inventory in the appendix. After you have scored your gifts, target your primary, secondary and emerging gifts. You will then want to be sure you understand what each gift is and how it operates both in your psyche and for the good of the corporate body of your own congregation.

As you ponder the possibilities of using your God-given gifts for service, here are seven clues that may further help you identify your gifts:

1. Tell me something about your heroes and sheroes, and I will tell you something about your gifts.

   We often admire and appreciate gifts in others without realizing these qualities reside within us, awaiting activation by God's Spirit.

2. Tell me about your most meaningful and fulfilling experiences, and I will tell you something about your gifts.

God may choose to use great, high and holy moments to move us deeper into what God has for us in the ordinary. We bring back down from mountain top experiences blessings that will hallow our days if we will claim them. The spiritual gifts we need for continual transformation are often present if we will look around a bit while we are strapping our sandals back on and walking away from the burning bush.

3. Tell me about your delights and I will tell you about your gifts. Exercising your spiritual gift is not all dull drudgery. God draws us deeper into the concerns and causes of the kingdom by our joys and delights. Reflect on the rainbow moments that have blessed you, and you may discover not a pot of gold, but a gift ready to be offered in joy.

4. Tell me about what others consistently affirm, appreciate, and encourage in you, and I will tell you about your gifts.

   Often we are the last to perceive our own spiritual gifts, and we need to rekindle the gift in one another (2 Tim. 1:6). Let's get beyond prideful false modesty and simply own up to our God-given gifts so we can step up to new realms of service.

5. Tell me about the needs you most earnestly pray for, and I will tell you something about your gifts.

God often calls us through the needs that most touch our heart. At the intersection of the world's great need and our deep joy, we often hear a call to service. Seldom does a call come to us without the requisite gifts to honor that call.

6. Tell me about the shape of your burnout, and I will tell you something about your gifts. Elijah's wilderness "low moment" recorded in 1 Kings 19, reveals the gift bestowed when his journey was too much for him. The gifts of hospitality, comfort, and vision restored the prophet, and empowered his future service. God has spiritual gifts working through the hands and hearts of those around us, if we will be still. Hushing our noisy hearts and owning up to the sources of our burnout are first steps on the recovery road.

7. Tell me about your wounds, and I will tell you about your gifts.

   Like Jacob's dark wrestling match with the midnight angel, sometimes the wounds that come our way in the course of life offer more than suffering and pain. The healing path through our struggle may also reveal gifts that bring hope and wholeness to others.

   A grad student who was abducted from campus and raped discovered in the course of her own healing process that God's Spirit gifted her with extraordinary patience and kindly wisdom for people agonizing their way through recovery. Her capacity to come beside, counsel, and companion people made her deacon ministry a transforming experience for many with whom she worked. Her spiritual gifts arose out of her own woundedness. As you reflect upon the wounded places in your own soul, there may well be a gift and a calling at the heart of your healing process. Many have found that spiritual transformation contains an external ministry focus as well as an inner process to attend.

In working through this process of identifying your spiritual gifts as deacons, bear in mind your twofold purpose. First, discovering and operating out of your gift settle you into your place in the body of Christ, where you can truly practice your faith as a servant of God's kingdom purpose.

Second, being grounded in your gifts as a servant opens you to become a channel for spiritual transformation. Your openness to God's Spirit begins building relational bridges that lead to conversations and encounters that bring the kingdom to light for others. Remember the unique qualifications for deacons in the book of Acts? Acts 6:5 tells us the first deacons were persons full of faith and the Holy Spirit. What a powerful combination!

If you, as a deacon, consecrate yourself to God for the purpose of becoming a servant, please know that you are not required to accomplish God's work without

God's power. You supply the surrender, and God will provide the power and apply it to a purpose that matters to the heart of God.

In addition to spiritual gifts, God has given each of us many other abilities, skills, and talents. We can employ these in our service to God and to others. One of the best examples in the Bible of people using their skills and abilities to serve God appears in Exodus 35 as the Israelites are building the tabernacle:

> "All who are skillful among you shall come and make all that the LORD has commanded…He has filled him with divine spirit, with skill, intelligence, and knowledge in every kind of craft." (vv. 10, 31)

Abilities are "know-hows." They are all those things that we know how to do. We have lots of abilities. In fact, we know how to do so many things that it's sometimes hard for us to list them all. Our abilities can be used to *activate* our spirit gifts and hearts. As a deacon you may have the gift of encouragement with a heart for those who are unable to get to church for worship. Perhaps you combine this gift with computer skills, including desktop publishing and a database. You may use this combination of gift, heart, and ability to send a colorful and personalized greeting card to shut-ins on special days or just when God's Spirit prompts you to do so.

Many times we minimize our abilities or consider them too mundane or worldly to use to serve God. Second Timothy teaches us that all skills are useful:

> In a large house there are utensils not only of gold and silver but also of wood and clay, some for special use, some for ordinary. All who cleanse themselves of the things I have mentioned will become special utensils, dedicated and useful to the owner of the house, ready for every good work. (2:20–21)

Any of our talents, skills, and abilities—no matter how insignificant or routine they may seem—can be used in a deacon's ministry. When you signed up to be a deacon, you made a commitment to continue your spiritual growth in a lifelong progression that transforms your personality, stretches your witness and service, and reflects the image of Christ. This will mean becoming a lifelong learner. I don't necessarily mean "book learner," although I believe that leaders are readers. I mean learning to discern your gifts, learning to discern God's Spirit, and learning to apply your skills and talents to God's ministry. I also mean learning new skills to meet new situations in your church and in your community. Finally, I mean practicing spiritual disciplines of prayer, Bible study, and worship in such ways that you grow closer to God and become a person available for God's mission.

5

Finding Your Place in Ministry

The Hurrieder I Go, the Behinder I Get

How often have we thought, *I'm the only one I trust to do this?* Or *It's just easier to do it myself?* We are uncomfortable giving up control and asking for help. We use the excuse that it's easier to do it, because we're certain that others won't do it correctly and we'll have to redo it later.

When we adopt this attitude, we fail to recognize the gifts and abilities of others. We deny that often there may be more than one correct way. And, probably most significantly, we do not recognize that doing it perfectly may be an unattainable goal, perhaps even an unnecessary one.

The grace of God provides that even imperfect people are not only welcome in the church but required. Otherwise the church building would be a very empty and lonely place.

Many Members but One Body

Paul discerned the necessary role of the members of the body of Christ in 1 Corinthians 12. He speaks of the spiritual gifts as having been given to each member. He doesn't say that some received gifts while others received nothing. He affirms that every person created by God has a God-given gift, and those gifts should be used to glorify God.

Too often our churches have lost members because those gifts have not been recognized or, worse, have been ignored. Deacons are called to discern the gifts they have been given and to seek to help others discern their own gifts. The spiritual gifts inventory found in the appendices may help individuals and groups discern their gifts for ministry and service.

Deacons must learn to use their individual gifts as part of the whole. The entire body must work together in the same direction. Paul says that even the weakest member of the body is indispensable. Indeed the body that does not support the smallest part will surely falter.

If One Member Is Honored, All Rejoice Together

The diaconate is not a group of individuals; it is a body. It is a unity of parts and gifts held together by the

Holy Spirit. When these gifts and talents are united and backed by the Spirit, nothing on this earth can stand in its way or tear it asunder.

Paul says that "to each is given the manifestation of the Spirit for the common good...If one member suffers, all suffer together with it; if one member is honored, all rejoice together with it" (1 Cor. 12:7,26). Support of individual members of the body is vital. This should not be interpreted as a command to think the same or to agree on every issue. It does not mean that we must all necessarily enjoy one another's company or be best friends, but it does mean that we must respect everyone's gifts and the work that we each do.

The body does not necessarily work perfectly just because we each do the tasks we've been assigned or agreed to. Sometimes the body needs the help of a physician or a counselor. The body must be open to the help of others to make it work better or more smoothly. It must also be open to the Spirit if a change of direction is called for.

When the Parts Come Together as a Whole

Cars should be checked regularly to make sure they run properly. Computers that are clean and have had their hard drives defragmented and checked for viruses work better. The human body needs regular checkups to make sure that all the parts function correctly and that viruses or disease have not invaded and damaged the body.

Surprisingly, many groups of deacons do not feel the need to meet regularly. Those who are in constant, regular contact function more smoothly, execute their tasks more ably, and can find damaged or hurting parts more quickly before they become a larger problem.

Deacon groups that meet together regularly are prone to be more supportive and caring of one another. Individuals can see each other's gifts more readily and suggest areas of support to one another.

Those who study scripture and pray together will become stronger and more vital. The Spirit-filled learning and questioning group will be recognized among the membership of the church as a vital, powerful, and respected body.

Has Anyone Seen the Instruction Manual?

So you've taken the spiritual gifts inventory, and the gifts you possess have been affirmed by others. Now what? Certainly it would be sinful to possess a gift of the Holy Spirit and not use it, especially once it was recognized.

1. Question the Scripture and Tradition of the Church

    Learn how others who possess your gifts have used them. Ask your pastor or check your library for how individuals who have possessed your gifts in the history of the church have used those gifts. Discuss with your pastor, elders, or other deacons how your gift could best serve God and the church.

2. Pray

   Listen for the leading of the Holy Spirit. Scripture tells us we will not be left alone and that the Spirit will guide us. Be silent, and hear what the Spirit says. Ask others to pray for your guidance as well. A deacon is not alone; the diaconate supports the individual and prays for continued guidance.

3. Find a Mentor

   Look for someone who understands the working of the Spirit in his or her own life and who can help you see it in yours. A mentor need not be someone older or even more experienced than you. Simply opening yourself to the spiritual companionship of a fellow traveler may help immensely. Find someone who can help you stay on the path and who will hold you accountable for your own actions.

4. Be Open to the Discernment of Others

   Listen to the other members of the body. Question them as to how your gift might serve the whole body. You're not asking for other's opinions here; instead, you're asking them to open themselves to the Spirit's leading and guidance. The words of the Spirit may well be spoken by the person sitting next to you.

5. Be open

   Discernment is not a onetime thing; it is ongoing. Gifts may change, grow, or deepen with age and maturity. Listen, too, for when the tasks we are performing are no longer necessary or when others are called to help or even to take our place. A rut may serve you the same way a track keeps a train on the right path; but if the rut gets so deep that you can't see over the sides anymore, it may be time to change direction.

6. Do it

Procrastination is certainly easier than actually performing the tasks. Assuming that others will take over or that what we do isn't important is not being true to the Spirit or the body. The action or inaction of a single deacon reflects on the whole of the diaconate. Ask the other members of the diaconate to make you accountable for the work you are called to do. Set your goals, and make others aware of those goals.

They Don't Advertise for Prophets

You probably won't find a classified ad for people looking for miracle-workers, prophets, or those who speak in tongues. The tasks to be performed may not be glowing with neon radiance or heralded with angelic trumpets. (They might; God has used stranger methods.) More than likely the tasks will be harder to see with the naked eye. Those gifted with discernment may see needs that others walk by every day.

Ask the members of the church what they see as the tasks that need to be done to build up the kingdom of God. Talk to the pastor about the needs of the congregation. Discuss within the diaconate how the church can benefit from the efforts of a group of committed, faithful believers.

Don't be satisfied if no one responds immediately. We're not used to people offering their help and really meaning it. Ask often until someone takes you up on the offer. Don't believe that everything is taken care of if you don't see the things that need to be done. Tasks always need to be done and people need to be helped.

Dream big. The surprising thing about listening to the Spirit is that sometimes the ideas seem impossible. Yet the scriptures are full of people who were led to do impossible things, and they were always given what they needed to perform the job.

Moses had the power to lead the people out of captivity. Jonah, despite his recalcitrant beginnings, could go to Nineveh. The apostles, when faithful to the Spirit and when calling on the name of God, could perform miracles. Dream big. Nothing great was ever accomplished because someone thought it was too hard to do. Great things happen because regular people dare to dream big. When we fail to believe that the Spirit can help with big dreams, we limit our own ability to accomplish them. If we believe that the Spirit will fail us, we have already failed. The Spirit had nothing to do with it.

What? Another Meeting?

Most of us gauge our ability to participate in yet another group by how much time will be spent in meetings. None of us want to spend all of our time in meetings, especially if we feel nothing is being accomplished.

The diaconate should certainly meet regularly. Some business is inevitable. Serving schedules, training of new members, and assignment of duties are needed for the diaconate to work smoothly. Whether this is done monthly, quarterly, or on some other schedule isn't important, provided the work is done.

Yet this business is not what the diaconate is all about. In addition to regular business meetings, the diaconate should gather as a body for support, to encourage one another, and to help when others face difficulty accomplishing their tasks.

The diaconate should gather together to pray and to study the scripture. They should meet to learn what is going on with other deacons and with the members of the church. They should be discussing the activities of the other groups in the church and where they might help.

Members of the diaconate should be active participants in both the church and the groups within the church. They should be a conduit for information to flow between all of those groups.

A Diaconate Gathers

Being a deacon requires both commitment and discipline. Discipline is a spiritual muscle. The first few times you attempt something, it may be extremely difficult. As with any exercise, as the muscle becomes more accustomed to the workout, it becomes easier. After a certain period the muscle even expects to be worked. The more often you exercise a discipline the easier it will become; and if you skip a workout, you will miss it.

The diaconate, as a body, needs the same kind of discipline. The group, once it begins to meet regularly, begins to look forward to the activity. When the whole of the body is committed to the discipline, the individual parts will begin to look forward to the unity of the gathering.

How does the diaconate develop the discipline of regular meetings?

1. Meeting Date and time

    Whether once a week or once a month, establish a regular meeting time, both a beginning and an ending. Respect that time commitment. Begin on time and end on time.

2. Established Pattern

    Develop a regular meeting agenda. Agree on what you want to cover in each meeting before the meeting even begins. Agree as a group that everyone will respect the pattern established.

3. Honor One Another

    Respect the opinions and the limitations of each other. Truly treat others as you wish to be treated.

Respect the confidentiality of the group and the confidentiality of the members of the congregation. Act like Spirit-filled beings to one another.

4. Study

Use the time together to study the scriptures and to understand and discern the Word for the church today. Listen with an open heart and an open mind. Listen to the interpretation of others.

5. Prayer

Begin each meeting in an attitude of prayer and continue throughout the meeting as if in prayer. Finally, close the meeting with prayer. It is very difficult to be angry with another if you are praying for them, and it's hard to say harsh words if everything you say is being directed toward God.

What Happens When We Gather?

The hymn "Christians, We Have Met to Worship," 277 in the *Chalice Hymnal,* speaks of what happens when we gather.

Christians, we have met to worship and adore the living God;

will you pray with all your power, while we try to preach the Word?

All is vain unless the Spirit of the Holy One comes down;

Christians, pray, and holy manna will be showered all around.[1]

At the core of all of our gatherings should be the worship of the living God. It should be our focus both when we are together and when we are apart. Prayer is essential to the act of worship, especially when we are attempting to speak or act out the word of God. In both our words and deeds we should seek to witness to the word. Our very actions are a prayer when they are done to the glory of God.

As a gathering of believers, we welcome the Spirit into our midst. Unless we are bonded to one another by the Spirit, we are not united; and our accomplishments will fall short. When we are united and pray through our words and deeds, our needs will be satisfied.

[1]"Christians, We Have Met to Worship," words attributed to George Atkins (19th century), in *Chalice Hymnal* (St. Louis: Chalice Press, 1995), no. 277.

6

Encouragement for Discouraged Deacons

Perhaps because life is so daily and the rhythm of life in Christ's church requires so much energy, we who serve sometimes lose our way. It is easy to become discouraged by the demands of ministry as a deacon and want to give up. We feel overwhelmed by the needs and the requests on our time and psyche and give in to the anxieties and urgencies that finally sink us.

Like Peter's unforgettable experience of trying to walk on water (Mt. 14:22–32), attempting to serve Christ can get us into the most awful predicaments. We are inspired by Peter's courageous example of stepping out of the boat and moving toward Jesus. Too often those who could lead cower in the back of the church's sinking ship, bailing furiously and wishing out loud that someone would do something!

Focusing on the wind-damage and whitecaps while attempting to walk on water will sink us every time. The focal point of the practice of our faith must remain on Christ. Peter figured this out just in time to cry, "Lord, save me!" (Mt. 14:30) Peter was saved this time and countless other times by this cry. Up to our elbows in storms, controversies, and organizational dilemmas, we too must find ways to refocus our faith on Christ.

When seas are high and things get bad and you are thinking seriously of bailing out on your deaconing work, I invite you to keep in mind four ways that deacons can contribute to a solution.

The first way is to keep our lives focused and centered on Christ. We do this by actually practicing our faith. We practice our faith by practicing the basic spiritual disciplines. No substitute exists for daily scripture meditation, singing our faith, Sabbath rest, living out God's forgiving and reconciling power, hospitality, intercession, and generosity.

Scripture Meditation

Rumination is the name of that digestive process whereby cows chew their cud and move what they have bitten off and chewed slowly through their various stomachs until all the nutritional value has been obtained. When we meditate, we mentally chew the words of scripture slowly, moving the meanings through various dimensions of our soul and allowing every particle of the presence of Christ through the Holy Spirit to become the sustenance that feeds the soul.

Singing Our Faith

You may be surprised at how much of the power of our faith comes through singing the hymnal into our hearts. Sit down with the hymnal and hum your way through its pages some afternoon. You will find your emotions evoked, your memory stirred, your spirit touched, your gratitude enlarged, and your perspective restored by leafing through the hymnal. Something about singing our faith brings it home to the heart and lets what we most deeply believe sink into where we really live with God.

Sabbath Rest

Unfortunately, we often substitute food or frantic activity or some favorite addiction for the rest our souls so desperately need. Jesus had a reason for repeatedly disappearing from the disciples amidst a busy ministry. If Jesus did not honor his Sabbath connection with his Father, he would have been easily overwhelmed by the demands of a difficult ministry. Sabbath is not disconnecting from life to serve God; Sabbath itself serves God by putting our lives in order under God. We learn to rest in God, while God is at work in us. We cannot do God's work without God's power, and the power is directed by surrender to the gift of Sabbath.

Forgiveness and Reconciliation

Simply put, Jesus died on the cross so we don't have to keep crucifying one another. Among his final words were: "Father, forgive them" (Lk. 23:34). Among his first words after resurrection were: "If you forgive someone's sins, they're gone for good. If you don't forgive sins, what are you going to do with them?" (Jn. 20:23, *Message*) If the first and last thing on Jesus' mind was the reconciliation of spirits human and holy, what should deacons be about?

Hospitality

When Paul urged us to "welcome one another, therefore, just as Christ has welcomed you, for the glory of God" (Rom. 15:7), he must have known how difficult it is to find anyone to take the initiative and serve as a gracious host in the house of God. Deacons, we serve at all the tables in God's house in the sanctuary and in the fellowship hall. If you see someone you don't know, don't hang back and whisper, Who is that? Get over there and embarrass yourself trying to introduce and welcome. A deacon's ministry to strangers may even put you in touch with angels. (Heb. 13:2)

Intercession

I believe that the door to heaven swings open to earth on the hinge of prayer. Some may question how our prayers actually affect positive outcomes. All I know is that when the deacons stop deaconing and praying, coincidences quit happening. So many of the needs we as deacons move to meet in the physical realm can also be attended to in the spiritual realm by our prayers. In many ways, deacons' prayer work down in the trenches of ministry follows the frontier practice of the Shakers, whose motto was "hearts to God, hands to work." The rhythm of work and prayer repeats itself until these two distinct elements meld into one continual life of prayer.

Generosity

This spiritual practice badly needs restoration. Some prefer to call it stewardship; I like to name it generosity. When deacons are living out the generosity of Christ in their everyday lives, it changes the weather in their congregation. One major reason our pious preachments rarely penetrates the pew is that we don't have enough deacon leaders who are faithfully practicing, showing the way by example. When the deacons' devotion to living out the generosity of Christ is missing, you can almost tangibly see the dull glaze of apathy and boredom that has captured a congregation. Wherever deacons decide to set a positive standard for the giving of time, talent, and treasure, the congregation notices this outpouring; and generosity becomes contagious.

Deacons who faithfully practice these ways of honoring the presence of Christ in their lives consistently tell me that only by actually practicing these disciplines can they keep from being sunk by the situations and circumstances that take us all down. Walking the path of practice requires great patience, but we can only make the way by walking.

The second way a deacon contributes is by stepping up into those awkward moments of transcendent hesitation that occur in every church. Moments of conflict will occur and can lead to healthy growth. But almost every deacon will sooner or later have a "baptism by fire" moment like this:

> The gathering to meet the new youth minister was going swimmingly. Parents and youth were not on their best behavior or even in the best of moods, but both were making major efforts to communicate. Then, one of the parents became emotionally agitated and verbally negative and started spewing out insinuations and accusations, just being a complete, to put it kindly, equal opportunity offender. Everybody gasped, held their breath, and searched the eyes around the room. All eyes were silently screaming, *Somebody do something here!* Into this moment of transcendent hesitation jumped a deacon. An emotional train wreck was averted, and the conversation put back on the rails because a deacon was willing to interpose his or her body and voice an objection. Into the yawning gap of stunned silence, while others

were busy being properly appalled, the deacon stood up and stuttered until able to raise a respectful question about the fairness of the accusations. An agonizing silence ensued, but the deacon sputtered until the Spirit gave words to appropriately respond to the ambushers and accusers. Finally, folks regained their composure, and the conversation regained its equilibrium.

Praise the Lord and pass the ammunition! The deacons came through! A deacon's job is not to stifle critique, but to keep the conversation from turning destructive. Fighting accusatory fire with the fire of the Spirit can turn a "baptism by fire" moment into a "baptism with fire." No special postgraduate training in conflict management is necessary, only a willingness to "place your body under the wheel" in order for the conversation to gain traction. This takes grit. It also requires that we become a calm presence for God in our congregational life. Deacons are worth their weight in communion wafers when they are willing to step up into awkward moments and not just stand by with their hands in their pockets and watch a train wreck happen!

The third way a deacon can contribute relates back to one of the most critical of the practices previously mentioned, generating a spirit of generosity. By any standard, Jesus was a generous soul. His own life was grace-kissed. But more than that, Jesus constantly lived out of the overflow of God's own great heart for a world in need. The integrity of our work as deacons rests on what we actually *do* after we say, "I believe." It is possible to lift the generosity level of the entire congregation. This happens when God's people witness the connection between what we as deacons affirm verbally and the generosity of our lives in giving time, talent, and treasure. No congregation can ever rise any higher than we are willing to lead them.

This principle first stabbed the awareness of a deacon who heard this simple offertory prayer following the doxology: "Lord, no matter what we say or do, this is what we think of you!" He knew what he had casually dropped in the plate that morning. His seared conscience had to admit that he spent much more money pursuing his hobby than he did contributing to the church. In his sales business he knew perfectly well how this principle operated. He had demonstrated to his own satisfaction that his business would never rise above the level of his own devotion and willingness to lead. Why did he expect God's business to be any different? This brief prayer launched a long journey into discovering what it means for one deacon to live out the generosity of Jesus.

Our generosity as deacons either creates a ceiling above which the congregation cannot rise or creates a floor of spiritual and material generosity to build on. Our examples create expectations that allow for new altitude! As a deacon you may decide that while a proportionate gift and a tithe are biblical benchmarks of intentional giving, your devotion to embody Jesus' generosity carries you above and beyond either of these traditional goals. Many deacons have found that living out the generosity of Jesus presents the highest challenge to faith they have ever encountered.

The fourth way a deacon can contribute to the well-being of Christ's body is by being a ministering spirit. Deacons can ably attend in so many areas to keep a congregation healthy. Let's name a few:

1. Attitude

   Deacons can help shape, mold, and model the positive attitudes that create atmosphere and allow good things to happen or prevent them from happening.

2. Boundaries

   Setting healthy limits and appropriate boundaries on behaviors that are detrimental or destructive is not an easy or fun process. I regret to inform you that deacons are among the "designated adults" of the congregation. Sometimes this includes blowing the whistle and calling fouls.

3. Congregational Care

   Being part of the heart of the congregation and rubbing elbows with the members on a daily basis provide opportunity not only to know what's going on in people's lives but also to offer ministry and pass that concern on to pastors as well.

4. Directing Energies

   It is easy to get so enamored with the internal machinations of the congregation's corporate life that we forget our mission of being disciples who make disciples. The great commission (Mt. 28:19–20) has never been taken out of commission, so our mission has a clear focus from scripture. Let the measure of our success be the effectiveness with which deacons rally congregational energy around this mission.

5. Example

   Never underestimate the spiritual and moral power of a strong, positive example. When integrity shines through in everything deacons say and do, it lifts the expectation level in the entire congregation. When we believe in Christ and belong to Christ, God's power is working within us to help us become Christ for others.

6. Followership

   Great commission churches that have visionary leadership also require excellence in followership. The capacity to put wheels under the vision and make it operational is critical to the witness of a congregation. Deacons who follow well are in no way inferior to those who lead; it's simply a different yet essential role in the body of Christ. Without effective followership, the church will have no discipleship.

7. Greeting

   Welcoming visitors and members alike helps people sense that they are family, that they belong, and that a place is set at the table for them. Such welcome makes fellowship authentic. The quality of this connection is not only an urgent emotional need in this high tech and low touch society but also a determinant of whether folks settle in or become part of the passing parade through the membership roll. Deacons are the heart of the welcoming spirit of any congregation.

8. Healing

   Deacons serve the bread of Christ's broken body and the cup of his outpoured life. Deacons handle holy things, not only at the communion table, but also at the back table in the fellowship hall. That's where the unguarded truth of the heart is revealed. That's where healing moments are often rehashed and harshness revisited. What you pass out there makes all the difference in whether a congregation can move past pain, or whether they will remain stuck in a time warp that makes forgiveness merely a formality without soul.

9. Intercession

   Your prayers as a deacon on behalf of the needs of others minister in ways that make a difference. That's what people who are hurting and struggling consistently tell me. Many of them are sustained only by your faithfulness to call their name in the quiet, holy moments you spend in the presence of God. As you learn how to bear another's burden in prayer, you are led to learn how those wordless prayers translate into ways you can actually assist the people you pray for in everyday life.

10. Mentoring

Deacons come alongside those whose passage in life's journey at a given time is rough. You mentor by companioning people, with or without offering advice. Your very presence in their life says, "You can do this; God's power is already at work in you; just let it out!" This is the Holy Spirit role so necessary to spiritual progress.

11. Kindness

Practicing random acts of kindness in Christ's name is a rare form of ministry that is not soon forgotten by friends and strangers alike. If you've ever been on the receiving end of such grace, the warmth and blessing make a lasting impression. Deacons are ministering spirits who live out the mercy of God in deeds. No sermon, lesson, or lecture, however brilliant, can substitute for this kindness.

The E Word

Many of these practical expressions of deacons' ministry may find expression under the general term of encouragement. Here we are not referring to having a pert, peppy, upbeat little personality. The word in Greek is *parakalleo*, which means "to come alongside." It is related to the word for Holy Spirit, *paraclete* (Jn. 14:16, 26; 15:26; 16:7). Deacons are ministering spirits who come alongside others for blessing as God has "come alongside" them. This is the essential point of 2 Corinthians 1:3–7. Deacons who can come alongside another person and act for their own good are living out this Holy Spirit role of encouragement. Deacons have themselves received the grace of the Holy Spirit's ministry in their own lives and, in turn, can embody this grace for others. The encouragement work of a deacon can take many forms.

First, we can encourage by welcoming. When we "welcome one another, therefore, just as Christ has welcomed you, for the glory of God" (Rom. 15:7), we are actually living out the spirit that invites others in and receives them as family. Bringing outsiders and converting them to insiders, those who belong and have found a place at the table, is the work of evangelism. Sometimes welcoming will mean being a helper or comforter. Teaching is another way deacons can encourage. Jesus was a rabbi who pointed out the way. When we, however informally, point the way to the heart of God, we open up other souls to the renaissance of God. Our lives are preaching the gospel for others to live up to.

Warning may not seem like a warm, fuzzy form of encouragement; but we need it nonetheless. When we come along beside another and speak the truth about danger, we are deaconing. The word of warning is much more effective if we have built a relational bridge and earned the right to speak so strongly. But a warning at the very moment of danger is a word to heed.

Fourth, cheering is another way to come along beside. We all draw courage from a deep source when someone notices our efforts and affirms us. Sometimes witnessing to the blessings of life helps others count their own. Habitually dwelling on the grateful side of life reminds others that our lives are not "all about us." While cheering can sometimes degenerate into cheerleading, a strong word of rejoicing definitely restores our joy!

Fifth, helping is another way of saying, "Bear one another's burdens" (Gal. 6:2). Coming alongside struggling people, lifting them up, and standing them on their own two feet so that they can carry their own weight is the core meaning of the New Testament term *sullambano,* "to lift weight and help carry."

Finally, we engage in deaconing when we come alongside someone who is struggling to help the person make sense out of his or her life or gain perspective on a problem. Speaking someone's "language" and helping the person negotiate thoughts and navigate meanings are powerful gifts of ministry.

With these and many more aspects of encouragement operating in the church's life, God's people are wonderfully strengthened with grace and power! What do people who don't have the church to come alongside them do when their lives are in disarray?

The Eternal Work of Deacons

This little handbook has focused primarily on the temporal work of deacons. We have offered insights into the historic role of deacons, outlined the biblical responsibilities, and honed in on the spiritual dynamics that lie beneath the roster of duties. But this does not, by any means, exhaust the work of deacons.

In the gospels, we catch a glimpse of the eternal work of deacons; though, it is indeed only a hint. Our entry point is the synoptic accounts of Jesus' time in the wilderness (Mt. 4:1–11; Lk. 4:1–13; Mk. 1:12–13). Here we catch a hint of the eternal work of deacons, as the writers describe events around Jesus' baptism. His mission of salvation was acknowledged, empowered, and inaugurated through his baptism. Following that glorious moment of acclaim and affirmation, the evil one attempted to pull the rug out from under Jesus' ministry before he even got started.

We've all labored through those Lenten sermons on the three temptations of Christ and how he fended them off. The critical piece of spiritual strategy is that Jesus did not blink or back down from this fray. Jesus stood surrounded by desert solitude, dark doubts, glittering illusions, urgent physical needs, and lies shrouded in logic. All these things oppressed Jesus. He battled his ancient enemy with scripture and courage that can only be born of utter surrender to God. Jesus' soul prevailed but not without enormous cost.

Imagine! Jesus was just beginning his earthly work, but he was already feeling the imponderable weight of the world's salvation resting on his shoulders just as he would later in the garden of Gethsemane. Teetering on the brink of complete emotional exhaustion and extreme mental strain, something happened that turned the tide.

In this extraordinary moment when time and eternity stood still, something made the bleak wilderness bloom for Jesus. Some presence made his darkness light. Somebody came along beside him and shored up his weak, wobbly spirit. Somebody communicated emotional energy and helped to heal the purpose of Jesus' life that was bruised and brutalized by the spiritual battle. Somebody celebrated God's victory, the first of many in his earthly ministry. Somebody brought the joy of heaven to earth that day. This sacred moment revealed the Source and set the pace for his whole ministry. Mark only offers this hint: "and the angels waited on him" (Mk. 1:13).

Now angels are ministering spirits, created beings of a higher order, whose energies are ceaselessly offered up to God in praise. According to John's apocalyptic vision, these heavenly hosts surround the throne of God (symbolizing the mystic divine center of the universe) and bear the music of majesty and might, honor, glory, and blessing before God day and night (Rev. 5:11–12).

They also serve as divine messengers, bearers of God's tidings, whisperers of God's will, energizers of God's power, encouragers of failing fortitude, revealers of the divine purpose, and revelers in the victory of God.

Here's the kicker. The word Mark uses to describe the angels' role in strengthening Jesus is the same word that is used to describe what deacons do. The text literally says, "and the angels came to Jesus and (deaconed) him." The Greek word is *diakoneo,* which has a range of meanings from "to serve as an attendant," "to wait upon (menially)," or "to minister as a host," in other words to act as a deacon!

Deacons, what an astonishing honor is yours, to "deacon" the servants of Christ as the angels "deaconed" Jesus!

Know Your Gifts

A SPIRITUAL GIFTS INVENTORY TO HELP YOU DETERMINE YOUR GOD-GIVEN SPIRITUAL GIFTS

The following Spiritual Gifts Inventory has been developed to help and encourage you to know and use your God-given gifts for performing the ministry of Jesus Christ. This inventory will help you to understand your strengths in ministry based on seventeen special gifts of the Spirit alluded to in the New Testament.

1. Respond to each statement in the inventory according to the following scale:

   4—always

   3—usually

   2—sometimes

   1—seldom

   0—never

2. At the end of the inventory is a scoring sheet. When you have responded to all the statements, transfer your scores to the appropriate place on the scoring sheet and follow the instructions for scoring.

3. Important: Answer according to who you *are,* not who you would like to be or think you ought to be. How true are these statements of you? To what degree do these statements reflect your usual tendencies?

SPIRITUAL GIFTS INVENTORY	Always (4)	Usually (3)	Sometimes (2)	Seldom (1)	Never (0)
1. I have experienced great pleasure in carrying out the details of an assignment.					
2. I enjoy helping people, especially those who cannot help themselves.					
3. I share my possessions with persons who need them more than I do.					
4. I have felt a strong desire to share the gospel with persons who live in other lands.					
5. The idea of standing in front of groups of people and sharing my ideas with them is very appealing to me.					
6. I have experienced the privilege of comforting persons who are experiencing hurt.					
7. I enjoy talking to others about my experience with Christ.					
8. I can often see the consequences of actions.					
9. I have a special sense of knowing when others need my prayer.					

Spiritual Gifts Inventory	Always (4)	Usually (3)	Sometimes (2)	Seldom (1)	Never (0)
10. I find myself compelled to help someone I know is in need.					
11. Preparing food for visitors and guests who enter my home is a great joy to me.					
12. I enjoy sharing the things that I have experienced in an effort to help others not make the same mistakes I have made.					
13. I am generally more comfortable with ideas than I am with people.					
14. Understanding the motives behind another person's action is important to me.					
15. I feel that I can trust God to do extraordinary things in my life and have experienced God's doing so.					
16. People in organizations and groups appreciate my opinions and often follow my suggestions.					
17. I enjoy working with and spiritually caring for groups of persons.					
18. Working with ideas, paper, and pencils is much more exciting to me than working with my hands.					

SPIRITUAL GIFTS INVENTORY	Always (4)	Usually (3)	Sometimes (2)	Seldom (1)	Never (0)
19. I see myself as a servant to others.					
20. I enjoy giving money for causes I feel are important.					
21. I have sensed God's calling me to share my faith with persons of other cultures and languages.					
22. When I have questions, it is difficult for me to rest until I find the answers.					
23. Helping others to know that they are important to the church and that their efforts are appreciated is very important to me.					
24. Sharing what Christ has done for me personally is very important to me.					
25. I can see consequences of actions, and I communicate them publicly.					
26. When I hear requests for prayer, I eagerly and immediately begin to pray.					
27. Ministering to the sick and bereaved is very gratifying to me.					
28. I enjoy being host or hostess for persons I do not know.					

Spiritual Gifts Inventory	Always (4)	Usually (3)	Sometimes (2)	Seldom (1)	Never (0)
29. My guiding other persons in terms of difficulty and stress has often proven helpful to them.					
30. I feel very comfortable discussing important spiritual issues and their relevancy to my life.					
31. It is not difficult for me to determine if someone is doing something for the good of the whole church or out of a desire to help themselves.					
32. Responding to God's call no matter what the consequences is a way of life to me.					
33. Groups elect or appoint me to leadership positions involving decision making.					
34. I enjoy helping people grow spiritually.					
35. Determining priorities and organizing resources to meet those priorities are things I enjoy doing.					
36. Showing people that I am concerned about them is a basic part of my lifestyle.					
37. Giving my possessions to others is a real expression of my life commitment.					

SPIRITUAL GIFTS INVENTORY	Always (4)	Usually (3)	Sometimes (2)	Seldom (1)	Never (0)
38. When confronted with an opportunity to share my faith with persons of other nationalities, I am eager to do so.					
39. Studying books and sharing the knowledge I learn from them are important to me.					
40. Helping persons through rough periods in their lives is important to me.					
41. I am comfortable communicating the simple truths of the biblical message with others.					
42. The ability to see the natural results of something and communicate it is relevant in my life.					
43. I am moved to pray for others, even though I may not know them, and for conditions about which I know very little or nothing at the time.					
44. I enjoy looking for persons with needs and finding ways to help.					
45. I like to open my life to strangers and guests and help them to know that I care.					

Spiritual Gifts Inventory	Always (4)	Usually (3)	Sometimes (2)	Seldom (1)	Never (0)
46. I feel that I can help clarify the importance of decisions and events, and I try to do so whenever possible.					
47. I am aware of my ability to grasp significant ideas and truths of the biblical message.					
48. I have the ability to decide whether something is good or evil.					
49. I respond to my impressions of what God wants me to do even when under extreme pressure and great opportunity for failure.					
50. I am skilled in setting forth positive and precise steps of action.					
51. People express appreciation for the spiritual help they receive through friendship with me.					
52. Organizing projects and involving other persons in them are exciting to me.					
53. I enjoy helping sick persons on a continuing basis.					
54. Giving my material possessions to others is something I enjoy doing.					

SPIRITUAL GIFTS INVENTORY	Always (4)	Usually (3)	Sometimes (2)	Seldom (1)	Never (0)
55. I have a deep concern for persons in other countries and nations who have not heard about Jesus Christ.					
56. I enjoy planning and preparing to lead learning experiences.					
57. Using relational skills in counseling has been an important aspect of my Christian experience.					
58. Helping others understand what it means to be a Christian is one of my major goals in life.					
59. I can see where a decision will lead and share the outcome before it happens.					
60. I pray with confidence because I know God works in response to prayer.					
61. Finding help for persons who are in crises is something I enjoy doing.					
62. I have an ability to put persons at ease very quickly when they enter my home.					
63. I have felt that my ability to share important insights with others has contributed meaningfully to their lives.					

SPIRITUAL GIFTS INVENTORY	Always (4)	Usually (3)	Sometimes (2)	Seldom (1)	Never (0)
64. Gaining new insights into biblical truth is important to me.					
65. I find myself evaluating the need and/or importance of ministries in the church.					
66. I have been able to understand the importance of moving forward in certain areas of life even when I did not fully realize what the future would hold.					
67. I set goals and manage people and resources effectively to accomplish them.					
68. People often seek my counsel in personal spiritual matters.					
69. The idea of leading a group of persons to achieve a particular purpose is very appealing to me.					
70. Serving the needs of others is very important to me.					
71. The giving of myself to others is one of the exciting experiences of my life.					
72. Being sent by God to another state or country to share the gospel is on my mind.					

SPIRITUAL GIFTS INVENTORY	Always (4)	Usually (3)	Sometimes (2)	Seldom (1)	Never (0)
73. I find myself wishing I had the opportunity to share with others the things I have learned from my study and experiences.					
74. I feel equipped to provide encouragement to persons who need it.					
75. The thought of telling someone else about Christ is my greatest joy.					
76. I have experience in knowing the outcome of a situation before it actually occurs.					
77. I am honored when someone asks me to pray for them.					
78. I like being involved in meeting the physical and material needs of others.					
79. Opening my home to strangers is a good way to make new friends, and I enjoy doing it.					
80. I attempt to share my concerns and insights when the church is considering important actions that will have a great impact on the church's ministries.					

Spiritual Gifts Inventory	Always (4)	Usually (3)	Sometimes (2)	Seldom (1)	Never (0)
81. I enjoy the interaction of others when discussing ideas and issues I feel to be important.					
82. I think it is very important to test whether something is potentially good or bad.					
83. I have acted in ways that have shown me that I have ability to perceive what God wants before others have even thought about it.					
84. I am able to cast a vision that others want to be part of.					
85. I enjoy giving guidance and practical support to a small group of people.					

SCORING

Transfer the score you gave each item to the appropriate box below. Then add the total score for each gift and place it in the box marked TOTAL.

GIFTS	ITEM NUMBER					TOTAL
Administration	1	18	35	52	69	
Service	2	19	36	53	70	
Giving	3	20	37	54	71	
Apostleship	4	21	38	55	72	
Teaching	5	22	39	56	73	
Exhortation	6	23	40	57	74	
Evangelism	7	24	41	58	75	
Prophecy	8	25	42	59	76	
Intercession	9	26	43	60	77	
Mercy	10	27	44	61	78	
Hospitality	11	28	45	62	79	
Wisdom	12	29	46	63	80	
Knowledge	13	30	47	64	81	
Discernment	14	31	48	65	82	
Faith	15	32	49	66	83	
Leadership	16	33	50	67	84	
Shepherding	17	34	51	68	85	

Interpreting Your Scores

God is very generous in distributing spiritual gifts. Most of us have several gifts that we can employ in Christian service. To get a picture of your unique gift-mix, use the chart below.

1. Place your highest-scoring gift (or gifts if you have a tie) in the middle circle, marked Primary Gift(s). This is the gift you have indicated that you use most consistently.

2. There is usually a cluster of gifts on which you score relatively high, but not as high as your primary gift. Write these in the circle marked Secondary Gifts. These are the gifts that your inventory shows you use fairly often.

3. Finally, there are some gifts that God may be developing in you. They may not score high on the inventory, but you may feel drawn to them or sense that they are emerging in your Christian life. Write these gifts in the Developing Gifts area around the circles.

Spiritual Gifts Inventory developed by Dr. Gary Straub, First Christian Church (Disciples) 316 Ann Street, Frankfort, Kentucky.

Developing Gifts

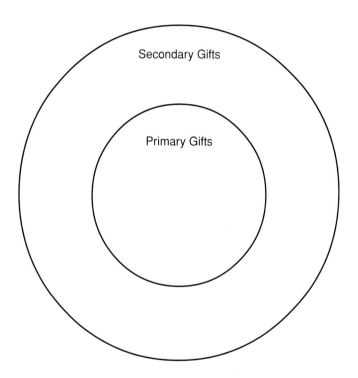

Developing Gifts